Real Estate Reviews

A step-by-step guide to using the Visual Pricing System to make a quick market summary that creates sales from your current customer base, in a simple and powerful method.

By: Tim DeLeon

ISBN: 9781791620998

Table of Contents

Introduction: "Trendbenders"   1

What Is a Real Estate Review?   3

Why Should You Do a Real Estate Review?   5

When Is the Best Time to Do a Real Estate Review?   7

How to Do a Successful Real Estate Review:

A Step-By-Step Guide   9

Conclusion   29

Appendix A: An Example Real Estate Review   31

About the Author   49

Introduction

What if I told you that there is one key process that many real estate professionals don't do that can massively impact their business in a positive manner? **_Would you want to know what that process is?_**

What if I told you that this easy-to-do activity could dramatically improve your business <u>in the next three months</u>? **_Would you want to know what that process is?_**

What if I told you, with minimal effort, this process would not only grow your business but cause your customers to respect and trust you more? **_Would you want to know what that process is?_**

"Trendbenders"

In late 2017, Larry Kendall, of Ninja Selling®,[1] presented a webinar on what he called "Trendbenders." Larry has spent his career working with real estate professionals on the goal of improving their productivity and their "dollars per hour." At times, Larry has witnessed situations where a real estate professional will be generating a specific amount of income (tending to stay at that level, year after year), and then for some reason, Larry will see them dramatically improve their income. That is a Trendbender.

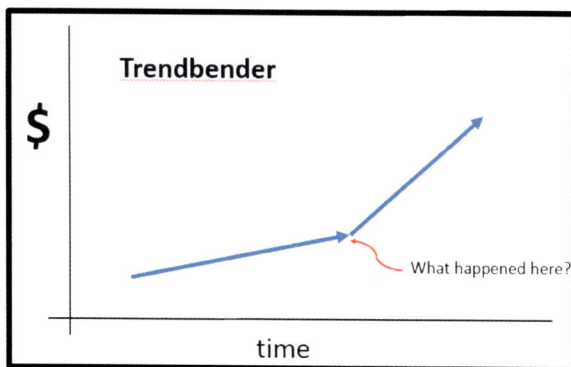

A Trendbender is where you have an uncommonly large change in your income or in your income per hour.

Larry is always looking for these Trendbenders, and when he finds that someone's income has dramatically increased, he's always asking, what happened? What was it that caused such a dramatic increase of income in such a short amount of time?

---

[1] Ninja Selling is a real estate training company based in Fort Collins, CO. To learn more about their world-class training courses and materials, please visit www.ninjaselling.com.

In that webinar, Larry identified the top ten Trendbenders he had found over the last couple of years. The second Trendbender Larry identified and researched was the use of Real Estate Reviews. A Real Estate Review, if done using a specific process, provided another key flow opportunity that increased a real estate professional's value and caused listings and sales to be generated from your current customer base.

__The Real Estate Review process is a powerful activity that causes rapport to be built, sales to occur, and income to grow.__

Larry found that the Real Estate Review was a simple way for real estate professionals to improve their business in three months or less, and matched with the Ninja Selling principles of staying in FLOW with your clients. He has been teaching about the need to be doing Real Estate Reviews across the world. Now, in this guide, you'll be able to join the masses who have learned not only the power this Trendbender has but also how to be taken down a simple, step-by-step, guided path to creating and presenting your Real Estate Review in a way that will cause your business to grow.

Before going into the step-by-step approach of "how" to create and present your Real Estate Reviews, we must answer three key questions: **what**, **why,** and **when?**

What is a Real Estate Review?
Why should you do a Real Estate Review?
When is the best time to do a Real Estate Review?

What Is a Real Estate Review?

A Real Estate Review is a powerful process for you to use, but what exactly is it?

The Real Estate Review is a quick summary of the real estate market. It should be short in length (six or seven pages, not forty) and brief in time to create and present (five to ten minutes to put together, ten to fifteen minutes to present). It should be customized and specific to that customer and give them a rough idea of what the value of their home is. Additionally, it should be the stimulus for them to think about the equity in their home and, with that knowledge, create the desire to take advantage of that equity.

We'll look at an actual example a little later, but first you must understand something about Real Estate Reviews. A Real Estate Review is a market summary for your clients, and a tool for you. It is a tool to put yourself in the position of a trusted advisor. ***You want to be part of the trusted advisor team.***

At the end of the year, I get a call from my insurance agent, who says that he'd like to go over my policies to make sure that I have the protection that I need. My wife and I have several investment properties, a few businesses, and personal residences that require multiple insurances that tend to change yearly in their demands. My agent's call made me think, and I realized the properties we own have increased in value over the last few years. As a result, I scheduled a meeting and increased my coverage to ensure we were completely covered.

Periodically, we get calls from our doctor, dentist, optometrist, and other professionals for checkups. We also meet and communicate with our accountant and financial advisor annually, during tax season. The list of advisors who call us to check in from time to time goes on and on. Every year, six months, or in some cases, thirty days, we communicate with advisors/professionals to set up meetings and do checkups.

What about real estate? Are you doing this as a real estate professional? Are you positioning yourself as a trusted advisor to your clients in the same respect as these other trusted advisors? This is the philosophy and the mindset of the Real Estate Review. It's also one of the reasons you should be doing them.

Why Should You Do a Real Estate Review?

Doing Real Estate Reviews helps you become a trusted advisor to your customer. But what is the actual benefit to you and your business? In the Trendbenders webinar, Larry Kendall talked about two real estate professionals he had recently met with.

The first was Maria Vitale, of LIV Sotheby's in Denver, Colorado. She had won the company-sponsored trip to Belize, which recognized the real estate professional with the most listings in a specific period of time. In talking to Maria, Larry asked her, "What was it that impacted your results the most?" She stated that she had a secret weapon: Real Estate Reviews. In January 2015, Maria did twenty-five Real Estate Reviews. These were all live reviews where she met with her clients face-to-face. *From those twenty-five Real Estate Reviews, she ended up listing fifteen properties.*

Larry also met with Joanne DeLeon, a real estate professional from Fort Collins, Colorado, and my wife. (Joanne has been mentioned in the Ninja program for many examples.) Larry asked her, "How do you have so many listings over the winter months?" Joanne said that the end of the year is her prime time. Many real estate professionals struggle during this "off season," but Joanne found a way to turn this believed "downtime" into "boomtime." From November 15 to December 15, she did thirty-nine Real Estate Reviews. Of those thirty-nine reviews, twenty were live reviews or a GoToMeeting™ (one of the many screen-sharing software programs that are currently available). *From those Real Estate Reviews, she created eight transactions the next month.* On top of that, she also had a number of transactions that occurred in the next year with her Real Estate Review clients.

Would fifteen or eight extra transactions benefit your business? *Of course!*

A Quick Note on the Market: We understand that in a depressed market, Real Estate Reviews can be a challenge. But with the market we've had the last few years, Real Estate Reviews are extreme Trendbenders. In this market, with all the recent gain, it's **FUN** to do Real Estate Reviews. Most markets throughout the US have had appreciation over the last few years. Do your customers know what they've gained in value over the last few years?

In Review: The Benefits

- Real Estate Reviews present you as the "trusted advisor."
- Real Estate Reviews provide an update to your customer.
- Real Estate Reviews put you in the position of being proactive.
- Real Estate Reviews generate transactions.
    - You should be getting a home sale or purchase for 33–50 percent of your Real Estate Reviews.
- Real Estate Reviews are one of the Ninja Nine.[2]

If Real Estate Reviews accomplish all this consistently, why wouldn't a real estate professional do Real Estate Reviews? In some cases, they don't know what it is. In other cases, they've heard about it and tried it out, but because they didn't know the right process or mis-timed the Real Estate Review, they didn't get results and then quickly abandoned it.

We've now briefly answered the "what" and "why" of Real Estate Reviews. Let's answer the next question:

When is the best time to do a Real Estate Review?

---

[2] The Ninja Nine is information associated with Ninja Selling and is copyrighted. It may only be used with permission from Ninja Selling (www.ninjaselling.com).

When Is the Best Time to Do a Real Estate Review?

There are several times in the year when doing a Real Estate Review has the most impact and greatest probability of creating transactions. Here are a few times when you should consider doing them:

- **An End-of-the-Year Summary.** We mentioned that Joanne DeLeon used Real Estate Reviews in the later months to create transactions. What we've found is that the best time to use Real Estate Reviews is in the November-through-January time frame. Why is that? There is just something about this time of the year. People are starting to set goals; they are thinking about the past year and the upcoming year. They are ready to plan their future, and that may include a home sale if they know how much new equity they have, thanks to real estate prices increasing. Real Estate Reviews can help educate your customers on just how much appreciation they have had, and help you become part of their future planning.

- **A Home Anniversary.** We recommend setting up a time do a Real Estate Review around the anniversary of when your client closed on their current home. A year-in-review-style meeting will show your customers exactly where their home value currently is and gives you an awesome time to connect and catch up.

- **A Refinance Request.** If your clients are considering refinancing, be sure to set up a Real Estate Review appointment. Before they pay for an appraisal, meeting with them and helping them determine if this is the right time to refinance allows you to step into the trusted advisor position and provide great value.

- **Pre-list Activity.** A Real Estate Review is a quick and easy way to get a base value before doing an in-depth analysis. When meeting with potential sellers who are thinking about listing their home, bring a Real Estate Review with you to show them roughly how much their home is worth. That simple action could be the difference between having a new listing and not.

- **Life Changes.** A lot can change in a year. People can have kids, get married, change jobs, or go through a slew of different life changes, all of which may create new home needs for your customers. This is a good time to make use of Facebook and to look for these changes. Anyone who is having a change in "pain or pleasure" may need a Real Estate Review.

- **Drastic Market Changes**. Another thing to look for is anyone who has had a dramatic increase in equity. Our rule of thumb is anyone who has had at least $80,000 to $100,000 of equity, especially if they were a first-time buyer or had previously purchased three or more years ago. If there was significant appreciation in their area over the last few years, they may be surprised to find out what their home may be worth today.

How to Do a Successful Real Estate Review

A Step-by-Step Guide

The Real Estate Review Process

Now that we've set the stage for the Real Estate Review, we want to walk you through the Real Estate Review process. This process will take you all the way through making contact to set up a meeting, to creating your Real Estate Review, to using the presentation scripts we have found to create the greatest results. However, I want to impress the importance of **LIVE MEETINGS.**

One of the key components, if not "the key" component, of doing a Real Estate Review successfully is to create an opportunity to be in the flow and to be the source of information **in person**. Don't simply send an email or mail your review. To truly be a "Trendbender," you must have a face-to-face and voice-to-voice connection. Real estate is a contact sport; it's all about making the connection, thinking about your customers, and thinking about how you can help them. Also, think about how they would like to know how the market has impacted them. Put yourself in the position of being their trusted advisor.

If you do a face-to-face meeting or GoToMeeting™, something will happen an amazing **33 percent** of the time. You may end up with a referral, a listing, or something else, but something will happen **33 percent of the time**. Some real estate professionals do a beautiful presentation and then only mail it out. Once you forego the face-to-face interaction or even the voice-to-voice interaction, your effectiveness can drop to about 2 percent. Then, if you decide to distribute your presentation by email only, you won't see many results at all.

Real Estate Reviews Results
- Face-to-Face or GoToMeeting = 33%
- Phone call – Mail – Phone call = 15%
- Mail only = 2%
- Email only = 0%?

NINJA SELLING

With that in mind, let's get into the step-by-step process.

Step 1: Setting up your Real Estate Review meeting.

First, you will make a phone call to your customer. The goal of the call is to set up an in-person appointment. Here is a script that we often use:

"As part of my service to you, I'd like to sit down with you and provide you an update on your real estate property. I've prepared a packet for you, and it will take about ten to fifteen minutes for me to review that with you."

Here are a couple of important things about the script that are important.

- We love to reinforce that what we are doing is part of our service as their real estate professional. It immediately establishes that you are a part of their financial team. This elevates you in their mind so that you are providing them a service beyond just selling homes.

- The next thing we want to point out in this script is that we are saying that we've already prepared a packet for them and that we've already done the work. This is an important aspect of the script. If we tell them, "We're going to prepare a packet," then they may say something like, "Don't bother taking the time to do that, since I'm not looking to sell in the future." However, if you let them know that you've already completed and prepared a packet for them, as part of your service, they will feel much more obligated to review that packet with you. Then, when you let them know that it will take only ten to fifteen minutes of their time, it really sets the stage for what the time commitment on their part will be.

Since our goal is to meet face-to-face with our customers, in many cases, we'll just meet over coffee. Now it's important that we do communicate with them ahead of time and not just say, "Let's meet for a cup of coffee," and then spring the Real Estate Review on them. Let them know that the purpose of the meeting is to give them an update on their home's value.

Be sure that you make it clear that this is a Real Estate Review and not a complete market analysis. Let them know that if they are considering making a move, you'd have to see their home and spend a little more time evaluating their home and the market before you could determine where they would price their home, and you'd be glad to do that for them if they wanted a more detailed idea of what their home would sell for in today's market.

Now that you have the meeting set up, it's time for you to move on to "Step 2: Creating Your Real Estate Review." You can do this using other methods; however, we at Focus 1st LLC exist to help make real estate pricing easier. It's the reason we created the Visual Pricing System for Real Estate, a powerful Microsoft Excel-based tool that simplifies many of the toughest pricing matters. So in this step-by-step guide, we are going to show you how to create your Real Estate Review using the Visual Pricing System.

Step 2: Creating Your Real Estate Review Using the Visual Pricing System

First, we are assuming that you have the Visual Pricing System installed. You can easily subscribe to the service at www.focus1st.com. If you haven't used the Visual Pricing System previously, it may take some extra time initially to get set up on it. Once you do, you should be able to complete the process below within five to ten minutes.

Step 2.1: Print the Previous MLS Sheet

Open your MLS program and search for the property address. There will most likely be an MLS sheet from the previous time this home sold. Once you have found that previous MLS, print it. That sheet will be included in the Real Estate Review, and it will be helpful in the next few steps, by giving you information such as neighborhood or area, among other things.

Step 2.2: Search Your MLS

The first step is to see what real estate is doing for the subject property's area or neighborhood. You do this by using your MLS to do a search for all status activity over the last two years for the subdivision of the subject property. If the subject property doesn't have a subdivision associated with it, do a search using the map search of your MLS and look for natural boundaries. The results of the search that you do should have about fifty to one hundred properties. This is just a guideline, and there is some leeway, but try to find a number close to that range. Once you've selected properties, export your search results.

Step 2.3: Open Your Data in the Visual Pricing System

Once you have your search results exported, open the Visual Pricing System and find the "Visual Pricing" ribbon at the top of your application.

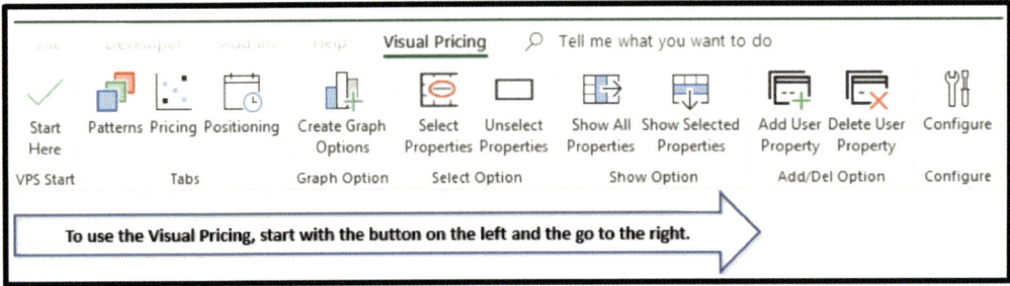

Located in the "Visual Pricing" ribbon, select the "Start Here" button.

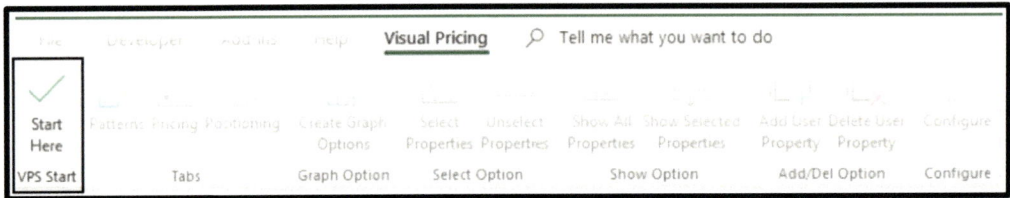

Once you've selected the "Start Here" button, you will see a dialog box that you can use to read in your export file.

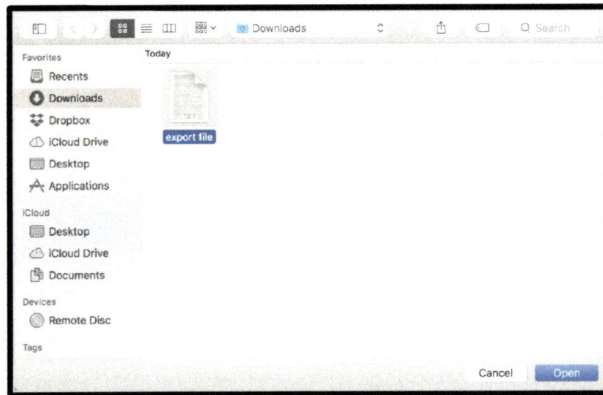

Select the file you just exported, and read it into the Visual Pricing System by clicking the "Open" button. Once you read in the file, a dialog box will pop up and show you the name of a subdivision from one of the properties it read in.

Provide Graph Labels

Please show the subdivsion / subarea
and the city you want to place on the
graphs. These will be used as titles on
the graphs that will be created for you.
You may choose any title you'd like.

Subdivision / Subarea Label:

English Ranch

City / Area Label:

Fort Collins

Done

Assuming this is correct, you can continue. If not, change the text in the box by clicking on it and typing the accurate labels to represent the search that you completed. Then press the "Done" button to continue. Many of the graphs you will use will automatically be created for you.

Step 2.4: Print the "Neighborhood Patterns" Graphs

Select the "Patterns" button located in the "Visual Pricing" ribbon to navigate to the "Neighborhood Patterns" graphs.

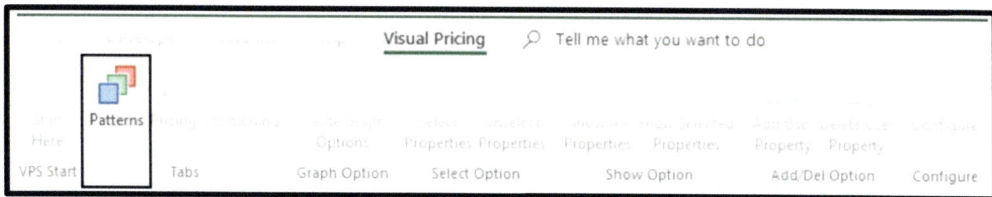

Visual Pricing   𝒪 Tell me what you want to do

| Patterns | | | | | | |

Once you've selected the "Patterns" button on the top ribbon of your Microsoft Excel program (shown above), you will see the "Odds of Selling" chart.

(See Next Page)

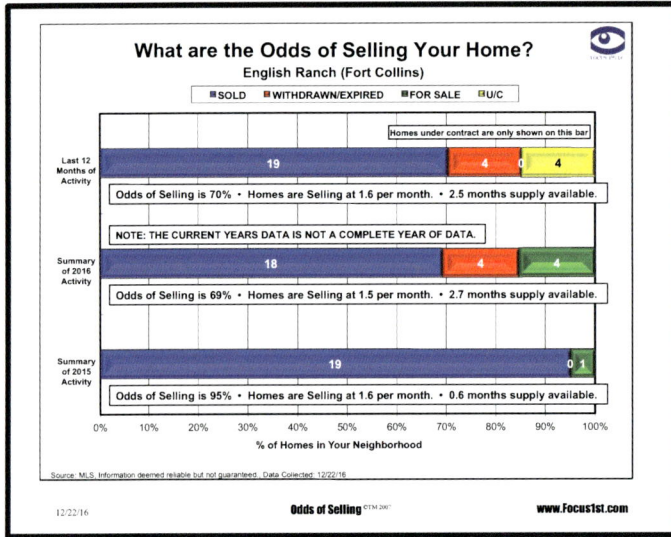

"Odds of Selling" Chart

You will use three of the "Neighborhood Patterns" charts in your Real Estate Review. Print out the "Odds of Selling" chart. Then go to the most recent "Time to Sell" chart.

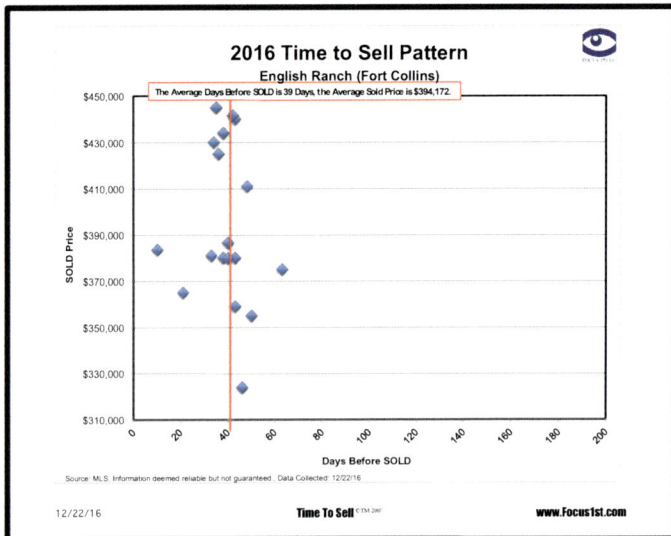

"Time to Sell" Chart

Print the current year's chart if there are seven or more data points; otherwise (especially if it's early in the year), print the previous year's chart. Then go to the most recent "Buying Pattern" chart that shows the complete year (or what is available).

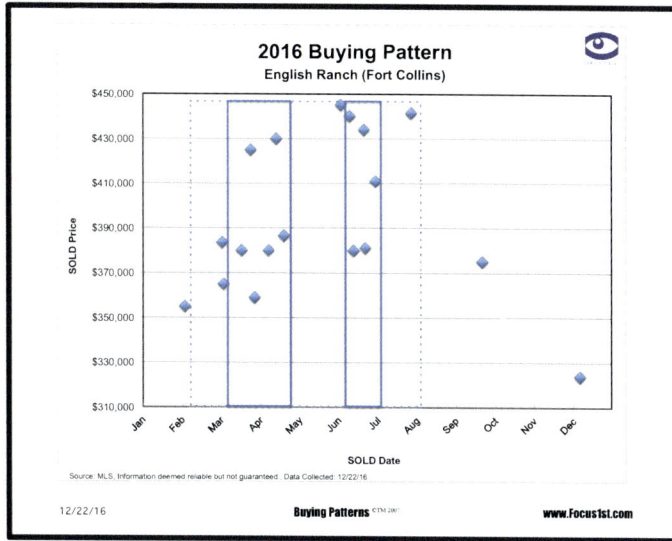

"Neighborhood Buying Pattern" Chart

Go ahead and print out that chart as well. These three charts will be included in your Real Estate Reviews.

Step 2.5: Create a Scattergram and Print It

First, select the "Pricing" button located in the "Visual Pricing" ribbon.

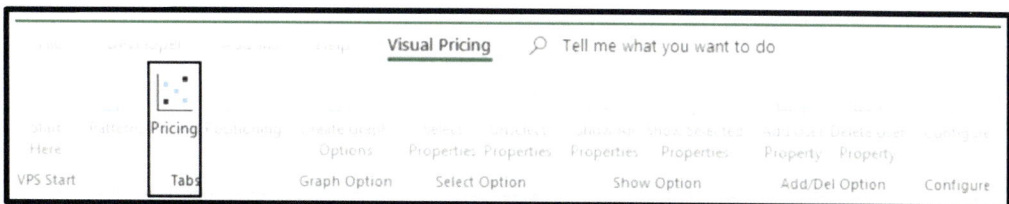

Once you've selected the "Pricing" button, you will see a list of properties. This is a summary of all the data you exported (all status activity over the last two years). To create your scattergram, you will first select properties and then create the scattergram based on the properties that you selected.

To select properties, we recommend that you select all properties that have sold in the last six months. The Visual Pricing System has a tool that will do that for you automatically. Select the "Create Graph Options" button located in the "Visual Pricing" ribbon.

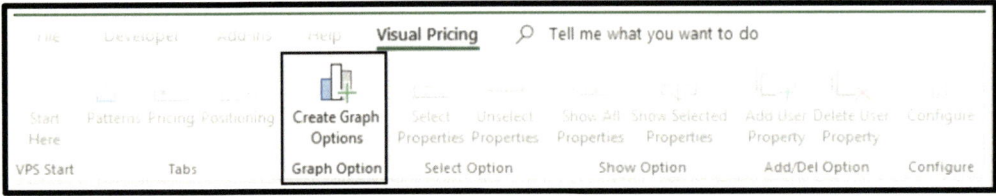

Once you select the "Create Graph Options" button, you will see a dialog box with several additional buttons.

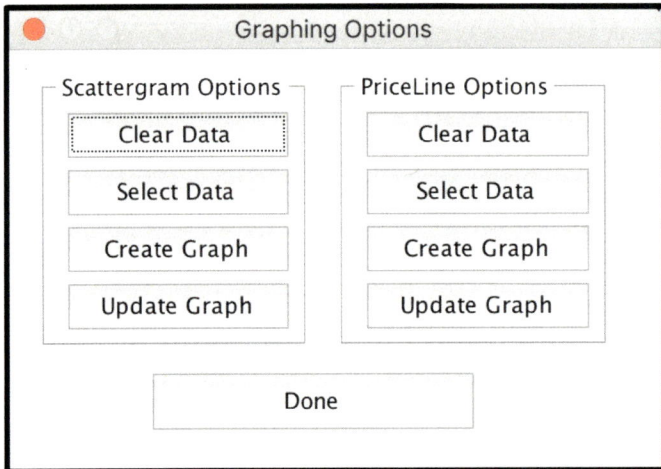

Select the "Select Data" button. Once you do that, you will see that several properties have been selected. These are all the properties that have sold in the last six months. Now that you have properties selected, you are ready to create your scattergram graph.

Select the "Create Graph Options" button located in the "Visual Pricing" ribbon again.

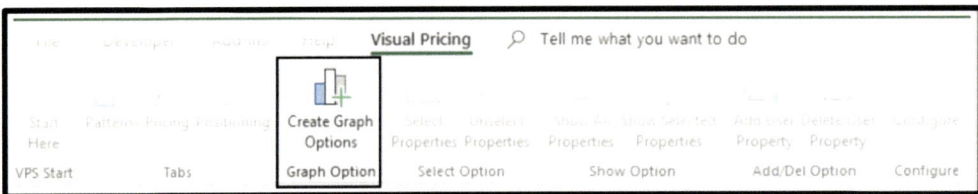

This time, select the "Create Graph" button in the dialog box and your scattergram will be created. However, before your scattergram is created, you will have the opportunity to specify the features on your scattergram.

We recommend that you select "Total Square Feet" (you may decide to graph "Finished Square Feet or "Above Ground Square Feet," if available), and we recommend that you include the "Trend (Fair Market Value) Line." Select the "OK" button to create your scattergram. Once your scattergram is created, you will see a new tab below, labeled "PSGram." Select that tab to see your scattergram. Print your scattergram to include in the Real Estate Review. Hand draw a vertical line straight up from the size of the subject property just past the intersection with the trend line (fair market value line). *This can also be fun to do in person with your customer as well.*

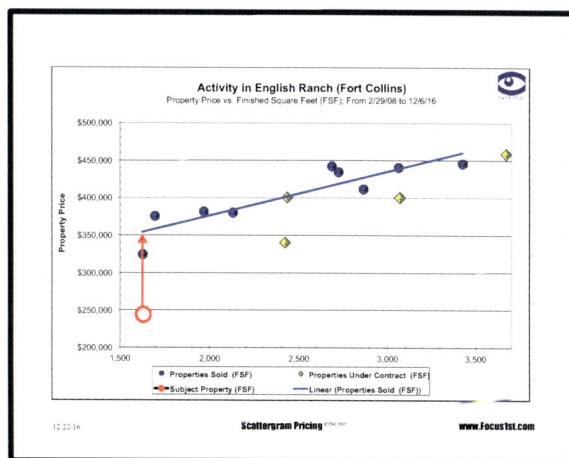

An Example Scattergram Graph

We recently heard of a study in which two groups of people had similar experiences but drastically different results. Group A had their homes initially listed at $600,000 and then later had a price reduction to $575,000. While at the reduced price of $575,000, they received an offer at $550,000. In Group A, 82 percent of those sellers who had received the offer of $550,000 accepted that offer. The sellers in Group B had similar experiences. They, too, had their homes initially listed at $600,000, and they, too, reduced their price to $575,000. And while they were at the reduced price of $575,000, they also received offers at $550,000. However, of the folks in Group B, 67 percent of them rejected the offer. So why such a difference?

Pricing Study

Group A		Group B
$600,000	List Price	$600,000
$575,000	Reduced	$575,000
$550,000	Offer	$550,000
82% Accepted		67% Reject

There was one minor difference between the experiences of Group A and Group B. When the offers were shown to the sellers in Group A, they were reminded of their original purchase price. So how did showing sellers the original purchase price impact their decision so dramatically? The key to understand the difference in behavior is based on what you're focusing on, or in this case, what the sellers are focusing on. In Group A, when the sellers are shown their original purchase price, they can easily see what they paid and the difference between that and their outstanding offer. For them, it is easy to see (and focus on) that they are gaining $150,000. That feels pretty good. However, the sellers in Group B are not as able to see (and focus on) what they paid, so they naturally gravitate toward comparing what their home was initially listed for and the offer they have. They can easily see (and focus on) that they are losing $50,000, and that doesn't feel good.

Pricing Study

Group A		Group B
$600,000	List Price	$600,000
$575,000	Reduced	$575,000
$550,000	Offer	$550,000
82% Accepted		67% Reject
$400,000	Paid	

So how do we integrate the results of this study in our Real Estate Review process? As part of the process, it is important that we are able to show the sellers what they had originally purchased their property for so that they can easily see (and focus on) their potential gain.

Note: While this is not necessary, an additional option is to add the subject property to the graph. You can use the procedure below to add the subject property to a scattergram if you wish. To add a property, be sure that you have the "Pricing" data (the one-line property description) up front. Once you do that, select one of the rows in the data, and then select the "Add User Property" button located in the "Visual Pricing" ribbon.

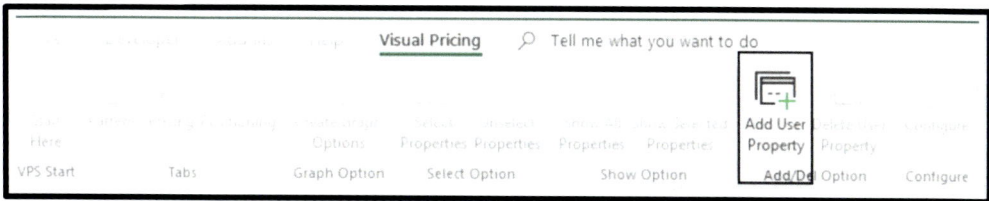

Once you select "Add User Property," you will see a dialog box like that shown below.

You can enter the address of the subject property, and then be sure to select "Subject" as the status of the property. This will allow the Visual Pricing System to highlight this property. Once you've entered this information, select the "OK" button.

You can now enter additional values directly into the spreadsheet. To graph the property, you will need to add the "total square feet" and the price (under "List Price") under the appropriate columns. We recommend that you enter the price of the property where it was when the current owners purchased it. This will be able to show them visually the additional equity they may have in their home when you create the graph. Using the "Create Graph Options" button and then the "Create Graph" button, create your graph. The subject property will now be on the graph, showing where it was when it was purchased by the current owner.

Go ahead and close the Visual Pricing System. You have now completed your Real Estate Review. There are a few more "boilerplate" or standard pages that you will add to each of your Real Estate Reviews.

Step 2.6: Print the FHFA Graph for Your Area

The FHFA graphs are charts that have been created based on data provided by the www.fhfa.gov site. It provides the most accurate appreciation for metropolitan statistical areas, or MSA for short. We suggest that you include the FHFA graph for the MSA for your location to show from a higher view what real estate has been doing near your area. Be aware that the graphs shown are for the larger metropolitan areas. The graphs for 325 metropolitan areas are available on the Focus 1st LLC membership site. To find an appreciation chart for the MSA near your area,

- go to www.focus1st.com;
- select the "My Account" link in the top right to navigate to your Focus 1st customer account login page;
- log into your Focus 1st account;
- select the "Appreciation Charts" tab to navigate to FHFA appreciation charts;
- select the link to your MSA chart closest to your area; and
- print out the appropriate MSA chart to include in your Real Estate Review.

Step 2.7: Print the "How to Read the Attached Graphs" Sheet.

Visit the following link to download and print the "How to Read the Attached Graphs" sheet. This simple document will allow your customers to understand your Real Estate Review on their own after taking it home with them.

http://bit.ly/RE-Review

Step 2.8: Write Your Cover Letter

Although you will be presenting the Real Estate Review in person (as we mentioned, you get the best results this way), it's still recommended that you include a cover letter. Your customers will appreciate it, and the neighbors they show it to will see your name and know you're the person to call about their neighborhood. Your letter should be short and to the point. It should include the following:

- Hello/Greeting
- Address of the home
- "Helpful for your planning"
- "Give you an idea of value"
- Invitation for a full CMA
- Instructions on reading the graphs

Here is an example paragraph that you may want to start with. Once you get your cover letter how you like it, it can be used for all your Real Estate Reviews.

Dear Mr. Green,

Attached is an update on your real estate located at 1001 Street Address. I felt that you might find the enclosed information helpful as you consider your financial planning. It will be helpful if you're considering getting a home equity loan, removing any private mortgage insurance you may have on your loan, completing a 1031 tax exchange, contemplating a move, or just figuring out your current net worth.

The data I'm providing should give you an indication of what's going on in today's market. The enclosed graphs will also give you a sense of the value of your home. Of course, if you need a more accurate idea of what your home is worth in today's market, I'd be glad to do a complete market analysis for you. Just let me know.

I know you'll find these graphs informative and helpful.

Your Real Estate Professional,

Tim DeLeon

Step 2.9: Put Your Real Estate Review Together

Here is the order that we recommend for putting your Real Estate Review together.

1. Cover letter
2. Previous MLS sheet
3. "How to Read the Attached Graphs" sheet
4. FHFA chart
5. "Odds of Selling" chart
6. "Time to Sell" chart
7. "Buying Pattern" chart
8. Scattergram chart

Now that you're done with Step 2 and finished putting your Real Estate Review together, you're ready to meet with your clients. Once you meet with them, walk through the graphs by showing them all the key aspects of the review. Here's the way we do it.

Step 3: Presenting Your Real Estate Review

The best way to walk through the scripts is to reference the charts in your Real Estate Review. Of course, the specifics of what we say are dependent on the actual data that is shown. You'll want to customize what you say based on the results that you are showing. But the scripts below are a great place to start. I'm going to lead you through an actual review I did.

**As you read through the scripts associated with each page of our Real Estate Reviews guide, you may find yourself wanting to look at the graphs and pages in better detail. Full-size graphs and pages are available at the back of this book in Appendix A. **

<u>Cover Letter</u>

"We have a handful of charts that I'd like to walk you through. I've put them together in a short report for your convenience. The first page summarizes that this is a real estate report and that the goal of the real estate report is to provide you with a quick analysis of the value of your real estate. It is not meant to be a complete and thorough market analysis. If you are considering selling your home or if you'd like to have a more accurate analysis, I'd be glad to do that for you. Just let me know."

Previous MLS Sheet

"The second page is a detailed MLS sheet for your home. This is the detailed MLS sheet that was available when you purchased your home. Of course, it was based on what your home was like when you purchased it, and a lot may have changed since then. However, in most cases, the size of your home is probably still the same, along with some of the key attributes. As you will see, we are basing the results on the size of your home as shown in this MLS sheet."

"How to Read the Attached Graphs" Sheet

"The third page is a summary of the upcoming graphs to help you understand them. Now I'll be walking through those graphs, so you won't need this summary right now. However, once we're done and if you decide to look back at those graphs, this summary may come in handy."

FHFA Appreciation Chart

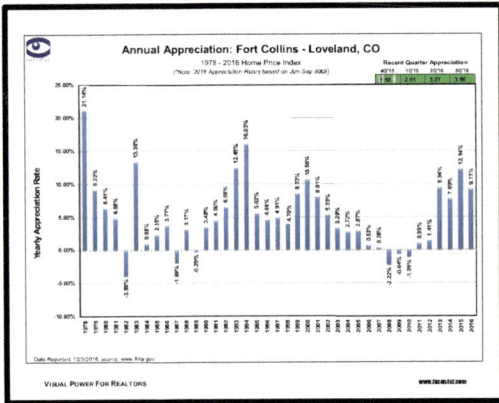

"The next page is a summary of the appreciation for your area over the last few years. It is based on data collected and analyzed by the government over the last thirty years. We believe that it is the most accurate measure of appreciation available. Look closely to see what's been happening in your area since you purchased your home."

(Note that since the appreciation charts are based on government-identified metropolitan statistical areas, also referred to as MSAs, it is possible that the subject property may not be in the specific area. If so, just let them know that you are showing the appreciation for an MSA that is near their location, just as a reference point).

"Odds of Selling" Chart

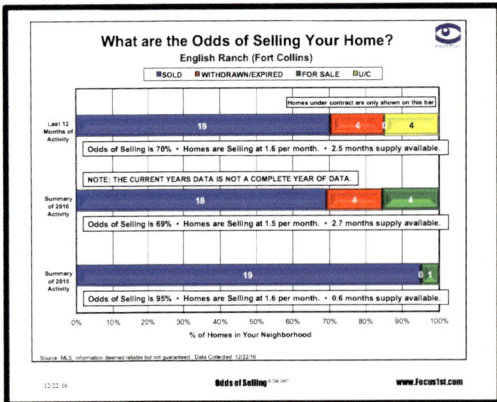

"The next page is the 'Odds of Selling' graph. As you will see, the next set of graphs are meant to show you what your experience may be if you decide to sell your home in the current real estate market. This first graph is what we refer to as the 'Odds of Selling' graph. It is a summary of all the real estate activity in your area, which matches your customer profile, over the last few years.

"As you can see, this first bar graph shows all the real estate activity for 2015, the second bar graph shows all the real estate activity for 2016, and the top bar graph shows all the real estate activity for the last twelve months. In blue, we show all the homes that have sold for each period. In red, we show all the properties that have withdrawn or expired. These are the properties that didn't sell for the value they had and for where they were priced. In green, we show all the properties that were for sale at the end of the period. Everything that was listed had to fall into one of these three categories; it was either sold, taken off the market because it could not sell, or still for sale at the end of the period. On the top graph, we also show the properties that are currently for sale and under contract.

"As you can see from this top graph, 70 percent of the homes that have been on the market in the last twelve months have sold, which is to say if we drove around your neighborhood and saw ten homes for sale, seven of these would be sold over the year. This is good. In cases, where the odds of selling are 30 percent or less, it means that this is a difficult time to sell. If the odds of selling are 60 percent or more, it is going to be a solid time to sell. Once the odds of selling get to be around 70 percent and above, homes are starting to sell off the shelf. For this area, if you were to sell your home, with the odds at 70 percent, we should be able to get it done. Also, as you can see from the top bar graph, while there are four homes in your area that are currently for sale, they are all under contract. There is currently no inventory available in your area."

"Time to Sell" Chart

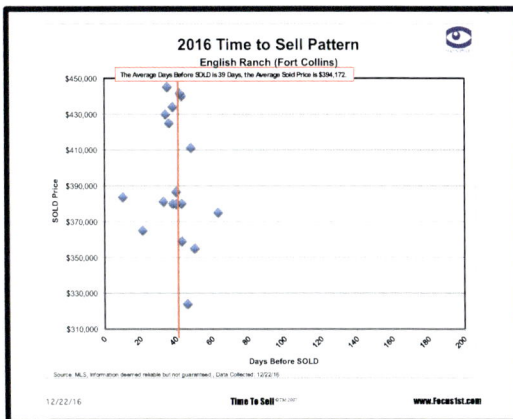

"The next graph is what we call the 'Time to Sell' graph. This graph shows all the homes that sold in 2016. On the left, we show the sold price, and at the bottom, we are plotting the days before sold. This is the number of days it took to close on a property after it was listed. The graph also has a red line, showing the average days before SOLD.

"We like to call the area before the red line the 'red zone.' This is comparable to the football vernacular that when the offensive team is inside the twenty-yard line, they must score. If they are inside the twenty-yard line and they do not score, they may lose the game. This is the same with this area in real estate. Most of the real estate activity will occur in the red zone. Here is where you'll get most of your real estate activity and where you'll get your best offers. Now, the data that we show are closed dates. Usually it takes anywhere from four to six weeks to close once you go under contract, so we can back up four to six weeks to get an idea when you need to go under contract to achieve these close dates. Since the average days before sold on this graph is thirty-nine days, it means that homes in this area are going under contract very quickly. If we were to put your home on the market, we would expect your home to go under contract within the first week of being on the market. In looking at the graph, if you list your home and don't close within the thirty-nine days (shown as the average days before sold), *can* you still sell your home? Yes, you can. There is a property that took somewhere around seventy days to sell. However, once you get past the thirty-nine days and you're not sold, the odds of selling your home will start to go down dramatically."

"Buying Pattern" Chart

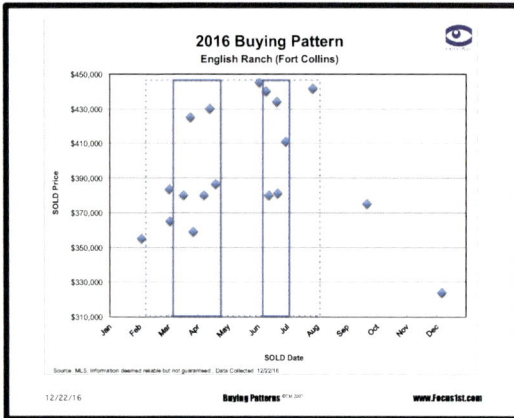

"This next graph is what we call the 'Buying Pattern.' This graph shows the homes that sold in 2016, and it plots the date they were sold. As before, we are showing the price they sold at on the left, and at the bottom, we have a calendar year, so we can show the time of the year the homes closed.

"This graph can show any correlation that there may be between the times of the year when homes sell for this area. The data on this graph is based on homes that sold in 2016. We don't know exactly what will happen this year, but if this were 2016, we would want to make sure that your home was listed in the first part of the year time frame."

Scattergram Chart

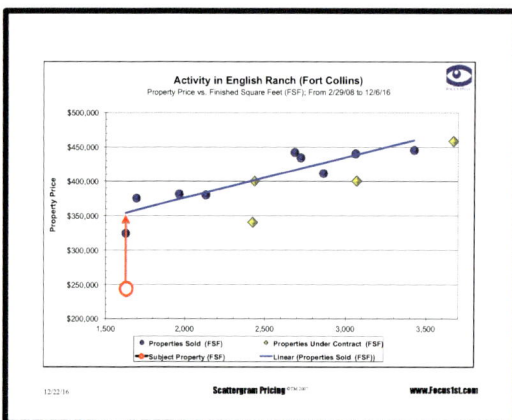

"This last graph shows all the homes that have sold in the last six months in your area. As you can see, we have plotted the price that the properties sold at and the size of each property. Each blue dot represents one of the homes that sold. For this graph, we've also included homes that are under contract as well. For those homes, we've plotted the list price (since we won't know the actual sold price until they close). As you can see, there is a strong correlation between the homes that sold and the price that they sold for. These scattergrams are great pricing tools. When we price properties, we look at five key factors, and you can summarize all five of those factors on one scattergram at one time. The most important factor is the location. The properties on this graph are located in the English Ranch area, so they are all in a comparable location. There may be some nuisances, somebody may back to a green belt, and somebody may back to a busy street. If these situations do exist, we can take that into consideration in the special feature and condition factors. The next two factors we like to consider are the price of homes that have sold recently and their size. This graph does a great job with those comparisons. And the last two factors that we need to consider are special features and condition. (Yes, I did already state that.) Special features and condition are what will move properties above the line or drop them below the line. As you will see, we've identified your home in the big red circle. This shows the size of your home and the price where you purchased your home when you bought it. If we were to place your home on the fair market value line (the trend line), you can see it would be near the $355,000 to $360,000 price range. That means, based on where you purchased your home (at $240,000), you have about $120,000 of equity in your home right now.

"Do you have any questions that I can answer for you at this point?"

You also want to consider how making a change could improve their life or their financial situation, so we recommend that you use one (or more) of the following scripts to leave them with the value of what a change would be, on their mind.

- "What are the long-term plans for your home?"
- "With interest rates starting to increase, are you in the home you want to be in?"
- "Has your home been a good investment? What if you had two?"

You may or may not get an answer from them. The important thing is that you've planted a seed. In many cases, people are just on the path of living life, and they never really take the time to consider making a change, even if it's in their best interest. What you are doing is helping them to pause, sit back, and really take the time to think about it.

Once you've presented your Real Estate Review and asked a few "seed" questions, you're done with the meeting. Be sure to keep your word and keep the meeting to the ten to fifteen minutes, as you stated. (Obviously, if the customer is spending time asking questions and is engaged, that may differ.) It won't be unusual for the customer to call back after they've had some time to think about things and ask you to do a more complete pricing analysis so they can consider moving forward.

Even if the customer decides that they don't need anything else in the near future, what you've done will have great long-term effects. You've established yourself as a professional, and you've provided a service. We've had situations where a real estate agent had completed a Real Estate Review with a customer and, as part of the review, left the packet with that customer. That customer had the review lying around their living room, and when a friend stopped by to visit, that friend saw the review and asked about it. After some discussion, the customer's friend was impressed with the professionalism and the Real Estate Review provided.

When the friend of the client decided to sell their home, they called that real estate agent and asked for a market analysis. When the agent asked them how these new clients had decided to contact her, they told her how they saw the Real Estate Review that was left at their friend's house and how much that activity impressed them. As a result, that real estate agent ended up listing a $3.5 million residence, the largest resale in her area at that time.

Conclusion

Real Estate Reviews are a powerful process for you to utilize. They are a great way to connect with customers, build rapport, and produce additional transactions. In this short book, you've learned what Real Estate Reviews are, why you should be implementing them in your business, when the best time to do a Real Estate Review is, and how to create your Real Estate Reviews in a quick and easy-to-present manner. You've even received scripts that you can use to get the most out of your time. So what's next? Now it's time to apply what you've learned.

I challenge you in the next fourteen days to look through your list and find clients who match up well to the sections in the "When Is the Best Time" chapter. Pick up the phone and call them. Keep calling until you have at least **three Real Estate Review appointments set.** Since 33 percent of the time, on average, that you do a face-to-face meeting, something happens, the odds are in you favor.

A lot of tools in real estate make grand promises. I want you to prove our claim right. Don't wait. Start searching your list, start making calls, and become a success story of Real Estate Reviews.

Sincerely,

Tim DeLeon
Founder of Focus 1st LLC

Appendix A

On the following pages is the complete Real Estate Review that I have referenced in this book in large format.

If you would like to practice your presentation technique using the scripts from earlier, or want to see the graphs in a larger size, please refer to these pages.

The graphs and charts are all part of an actual review I did of a property in Fort Collins, Colorado, a few years ago. I have removed specific property addresses, personal names, and phone numbers, but other than those details, this is an actual review that led to a transaction in my business.

THE**GROUP**INC.
Real Estate

December 22, 2016

    Wescott Ct
Fort Collins, CO 80525

      Attached is an update on your real estate located at   Wescott Court. I felt that you might find the enclosed information helpful as you consider your financial planning. It will be helpful if you're considering getting a home equity loan, removing any PMI you may have on your loan, completing a 1031 tax exchange, contemplating a move, or just figuring out your current net worth.

      The data I'm providing should give you an indication of what's going on in today's market. The enclosed graphs will also give you a sense of the value of your home. Of course, if you need a more accurate idea on what your home is worth in today's market, I'd be glad to do a complete Market Analysis for you. Just let me know.

      I know you'll find these graphs informative and helpful.

Your Real Estate Professional,

Tim DéLeon, CRS, GRI, e-PRO, NHCS
Broker Associate/Partner,
Office Direct   970 377 4942
Mobile   970 215 5579
Mailto:tim@timdeleon.com
http://www.timdeleon.com

Harmony Office
2803 East Harmony Road
Fort Collins, Colorado 80525
970.229.0700

"The highest compliment you can give, is to refer me to your friends and family members."

©IRES

Elementary:	Linton
Middle/Jr.:	Boltz
High School:	Fossil Ridge
School District:	Poudre

Lot SqFt: 8,179		**Approx. Acres:** 0.19	
Elec: City		**Water:** City	
Gas: Xcel		**Taxes:** $1,533.21/2007	
PIN:		**Zoning:** Res	
Waterfront: No		**Water Meter Inst:** Yes	
Water Rights: No		**Well Permit #:**	
HOA: No			

Bedrooms: 4   **Baths:** 3   **Rough Ins:** 0

Baths	Bsmt	Lwr	Main	Upr	Addl	Total
Full	0	0	0	1	0	1
3/4	0	0	0	1	0	1
1/2	0	1	0	0	0	1

All Bedrooms Conform: Yes

Rooms	Level	Length	Width	Floor
Master Bd	U	13	13	Carpet
Bedroom 2	U	10	9	Carpet
Bedroom 3	U	10	10	Carpet
Bedroom 4	U	13	9	Carpet
Bedroom 5	-	-	-	-
Bedroom 6	-	-	-	-
Dining room	M	12	9	Tile
Family room	L	17	13	Wood
Great room	-	-	-	-
Kitchen	M	10	9	Tile
Laundry	M	8	5	Tile
Living room	M	14	12	Wood
Rec room	-	-	-	-
Study/Office	-	-	-	-

PRICE: $243,500

Wescott Ct, Fort Collins 80525

RESIDENTIAL-DETACHED	**SOLD**
Locale: Fort Collins	**County:** Larimer
Area/SubArea: 9/18	
Subdivision: English Ranch	

Total SqFt All Lvls:	2050	**Basement SqFt:**	421
Total Finished SqFt:	1629	**Lower Level SqFt:**	345
Finished SqFt w/o Bsmt:	1629	**Main Level SqFt:**	444
Upper Level SqFt:	838	**Addl Upper Lvl:**	
# Garage Spaces:	2	**Garage Type:**	Attached
Garage SqFt:	472		

Built: 1992	**SqFt Source:**
New Const: No	
Builder: Bartran	**Model:**
New Const Notes:	

Listing Comments: Nicely updated home in popular English Ranch neighborhood. Close to schools, park & employment. Wood & tile floors. Tile counters, new appliances, practical floor plan, 4 bedrooms, 3 bathrooms, unfinished basement for exercise area/storage. New roof in 2007.

Sold Date: 02/29/2008   **Sold Price:** $240,000

DOM: 51 **DTO:** 29 **DTS:** 51

SA: Tim DeLeon   970-215-5579

Property Features

Style: Four-Level **Construction:** Wood/Frame, Brick/Brick Veneer **Roof:** Composition Roof **Type:** Contemporary/Modern **Outdoor Features:** Lawn Sprinkler System, Patio **Location Description:** Cul-De-Sac, Corner Lot, Level Lot **Lot Improvements:** Street Paved, Curbs, Gutters, Sidewalks, Street Light, Fire Hydrant within 500 Feet **Road Access:** City Street **Basement/Foundation:** Full Basement, Unfinished Basement **Heating:** Forced Air **Cooling:** Central Air Conditioning, Whole House Fan **Inclusions:** Window Coverings, Electric Range/Oven, Refrigerator, Microwave, Garage Door Opener **Design Features:** Open Floor Plan, Stain/Natural Trim, Walk-in Closet, Washer/Dryer Hookups, Wood Floors **Master Bedroom/Bath:** 3/4 Master Bath **Fireplaces:** Gas Fireplace, Family/Recreation Room Fireplace **Utilities:** Natural Gas, Electric, Cable TV Available **Water/Sewer:** City Water, City Sewer **Ownership:** Private Owner **Occupied By:** Owner Occupied **Possession:** 1-3 Days after Closing **Property Disclosures:** Seller's Property Disclosure **Flood Plain:** Minimal Risk **New Financing/Lending:** Cash, Conventional, FHA, VA

How to read the attached graphs?

I've enclosed several graphs to describe the market activity in your neighborhood over the past few years. Each of these graphs is described in detail below. Look at them and let me know if you have any questions.

WHAT IS THE REAL ESTATE MARKET DOING?

This first graph is a summary of the recent appreciation for your city. It is based on data collected and analyzed by the government over the last thirty years. We believe it is the most accurate measure of appreciation. Look closely to what's been happening since you purchased your home.

WHAT ARE THE ODDS OF SELLING YOUR HOME?

As you may be aware, not all the homes that are put on the market are sold. Some of the homes on the market do not sell and are either withdrawn, or have expired. This graph summarizes all the real estate activity in your area over the last couple of years. The homes sold, are the actual properties that were SOLD that year. The homes "Withdrawn/Expired" are homes that were listed and then taken off the market because they could not sell for the value they had with the price they were listed at. The homes shown as "For Sale" are the homes that were still listed at the end of the year.

HOW LONG WILL IT TAKE FOR YOUR PROPERTY TO SELL?

The next graph looks at all the homes that were sold recently, in your area. The number of days on the market before each property was sold is also shown. In summary, the average time on the market is a good indication of how long your home may be on the market. Generally, 60-70% of the homes sell before this red line. If your home is not sold at or near that line, your Odds of Selling will start to go down dramatically.

WHEN IS THE BEST TIME TO PUT MY HOUSE ON THE MARKET?

The next graph I've included is the *Buying Pattern* for your subdivision. This graph shows actual data for the homes sold in your area. There is a data point for each SOLD property that shows the date it sold and the price it sold at. You can get a good indication of when the best time for you to put your home on the market (and get it sold) might be. Be aware that these are CLOSED dates (most homes close within 4-6 weeks after going under contract). To take advantage these patterns, your home should be listed 30-45 days before.

WHAT IS THE VALUE OF MY HOME IN TODAY'S MARKET?

When we price properties, we look at five different components. Location, price of recently sold homes and their size, and lastly special features and condition. We can summarize all five of these factors on a scattergram. In this last graph, we are showing homes that have recently sold in your area and we've identified their price and size. To figure out what your Fair Market Value may be, find the size of your home below and draw a line to where it intersects on the trend line. This may give you an idea of what your home may bring in today's market.

FHFA Appreciation Charts

Recent Quarter Appreciation

4Q'15	1Q'16	2Q'16	3Q'16
1.58	2.01	3.27	3.56

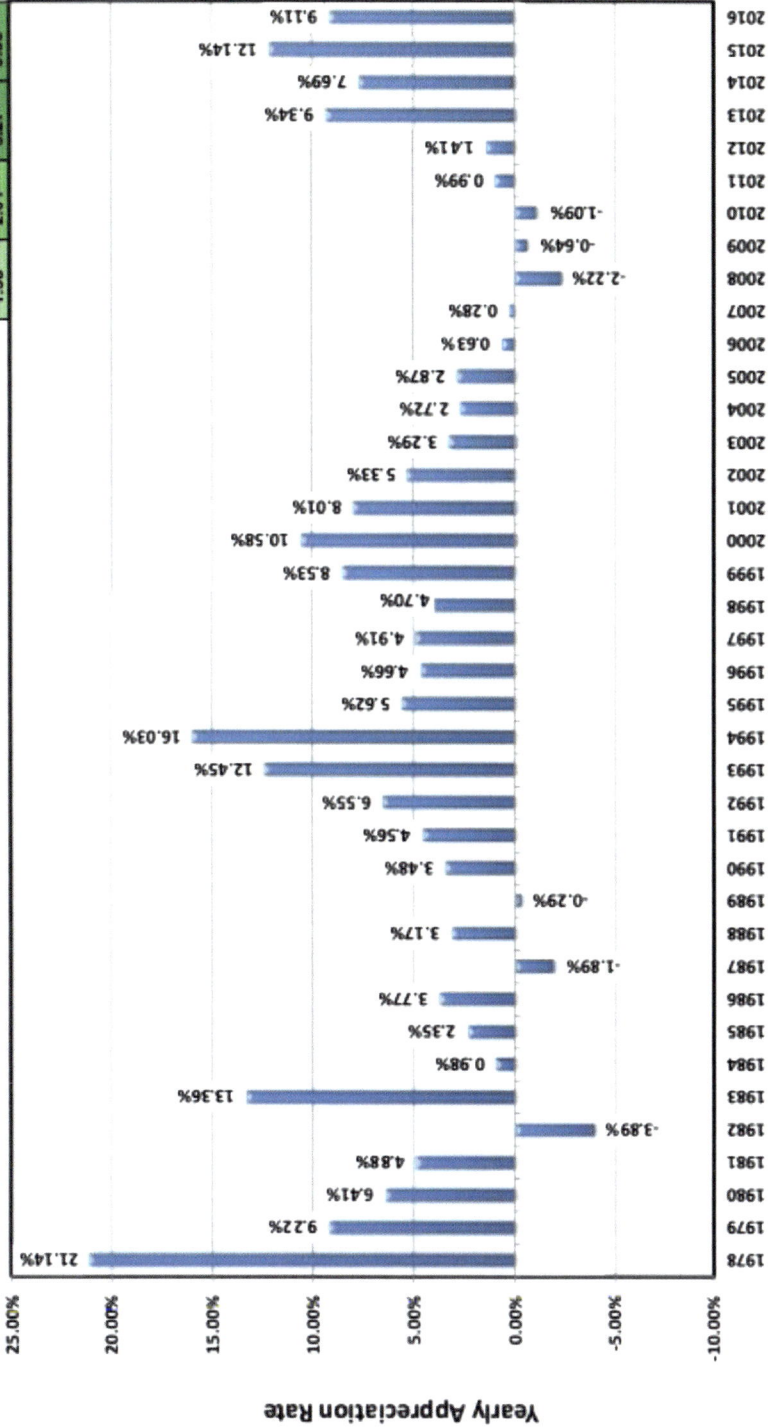

Year	Yearly Appreciation Rate
2016	9.11%
2015	12.14%
2014	7.69%
2013	9.34%
2012	1.41%
2011	0.99%
2010	-1.09%
2009	-0.64%
2008	-2.22%
2007	0.28%
2006	0.63%
2005	2.87%
2004	2.72%
2003	3.29%
2002	5.33%
2001	8.01%
2000	10.58%
1999	8.53%
1998	4.70%
1997	4.91%
1996	4.66%
1995	5.62%
1994	16.03%
1993	12.45%
1992	6.55%
1991	4.56%
1990	3.48%
1989	-0.29%
1988	3.17%
1987	-1.89%
1986	3.77%
1985	2.35%
1984	0.98%
1983	13.36%
1982	-3.89%
1981	4.88%
1980	6.41%
1979	9.22%
1978	21.14%

Data Reported: 12/3/2016, source: www.fhfa.gov

What are the Odds of Selling Your Home?

English Ranch (Fort Collins)

Legend: ■ SOLD ■ WITHDRAWN/EXPIRED ■ FOR SALE ■ U/C

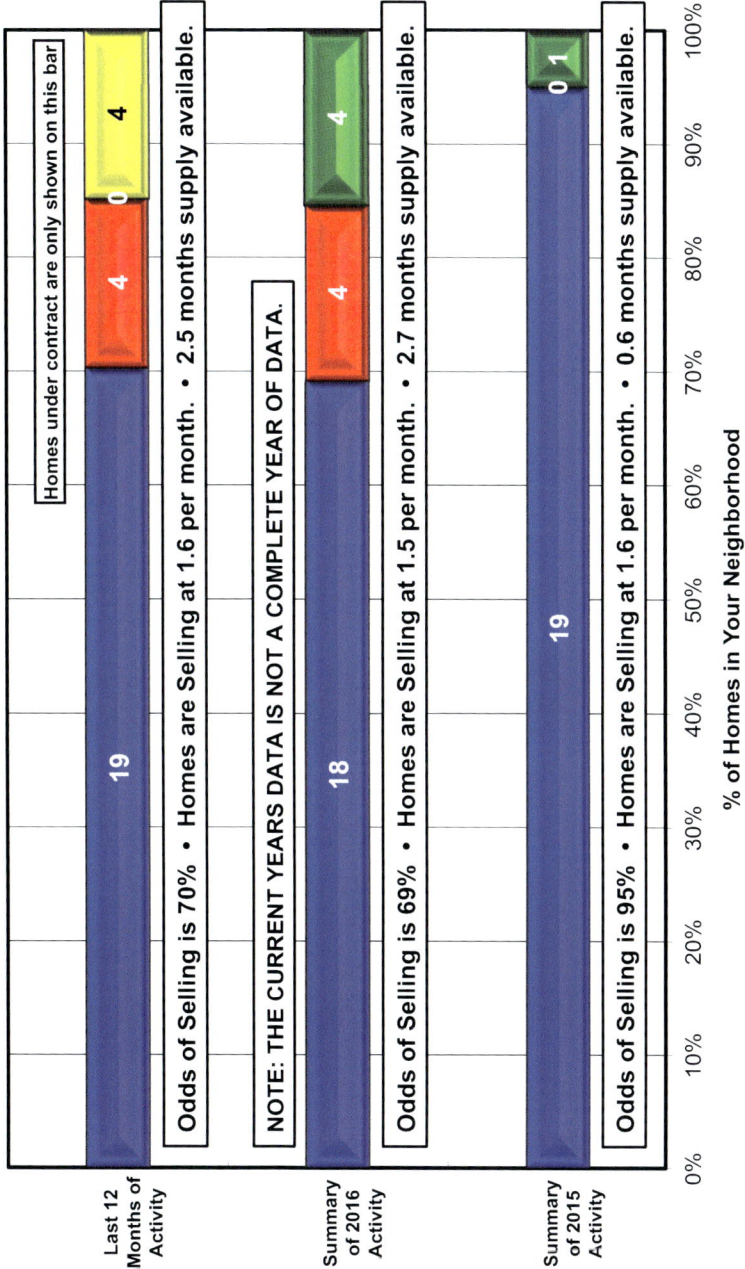

Homes under contract are only shown on this bar

Last 12 Months of Activity
- SOLD: 19
- WITHDRAWN/EXPIRED: 4
- FOR SALE: 0
- U/C: 4

Odds of Selling is 70% • Homes are Selling at 1.6 per month. • 2.5 months supply available.

NOTE: THE CURRENT YEARS DATA IS NOT A COMPLETE YEAR OF DATA.

Summary of 2016 Activity
- SOLD: 18
- WITHDRAWN/EXPIRED: 4
- FOR SALE: 4

Odds of Selling is 69% • Homes are Selling at 1.5 per month. • 2.7 months supply available.

Summary of 2015 Activity
- SOLD: 19
- FOR SALE: 0
- U/C: 1

Odds of Selling is 95% • Homes are Selling at 1.6 per month. • 0.6 months supply available.

% of Homes in Your Neighborhood

(X-axis: 0% 10% 20% 30% 40% 50% 60% 70% 80% 90% 100%)

Source: MLS. Information deemed reliable but not guaranteed., Data Collected: 12/22/16

2016 Time to Sell Pattern

English Ranch (Fort Collins)

The Average Days Before SOLD is 39 Days, the Average Sold Price is $394,172.

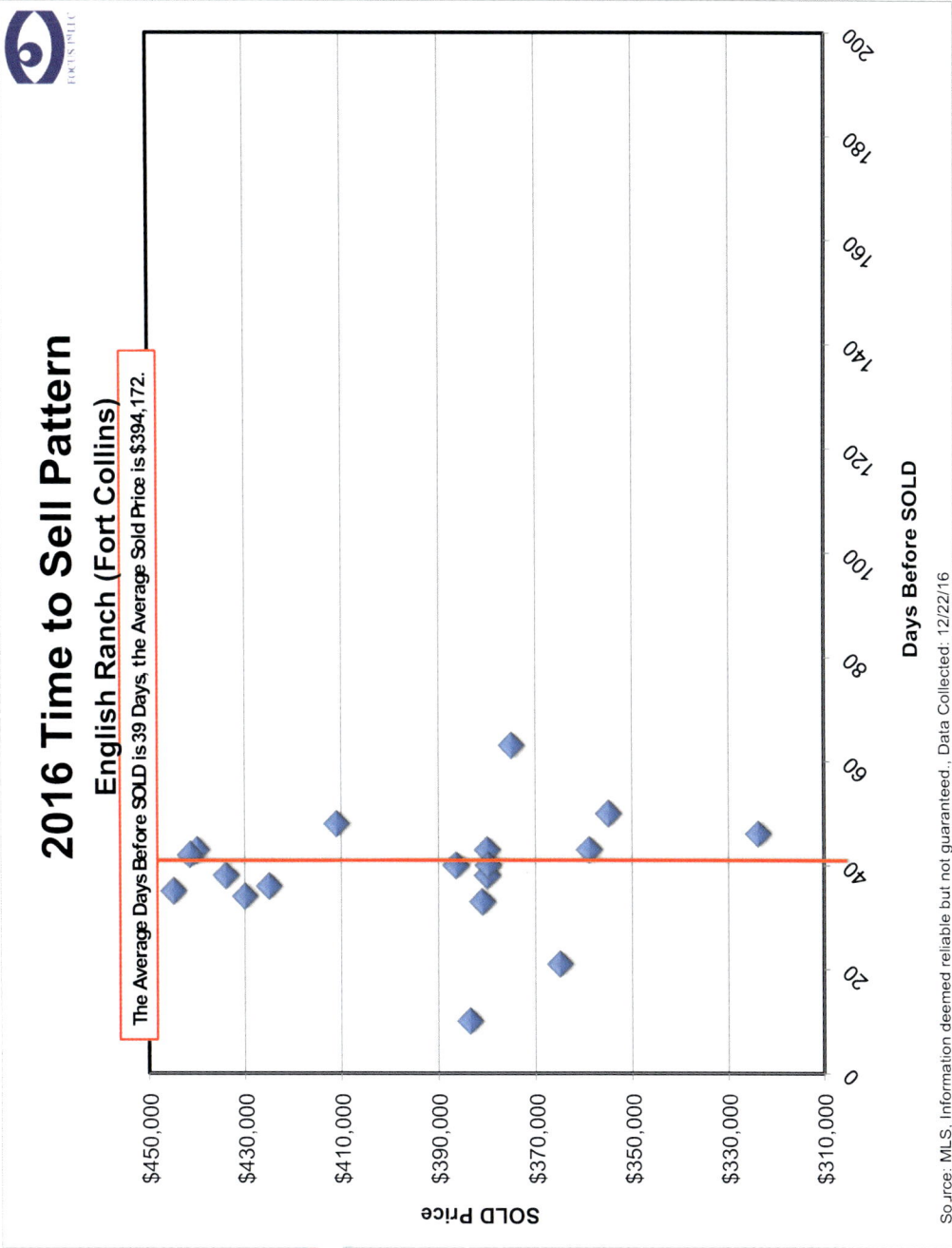

SOLD Price

Days Before SOLD

Source: MLS, Information deemed reliable but not guaranteed., Data Collected: 12/22/16

2016 Buying Pattern
English Ranch (Fort Collins)

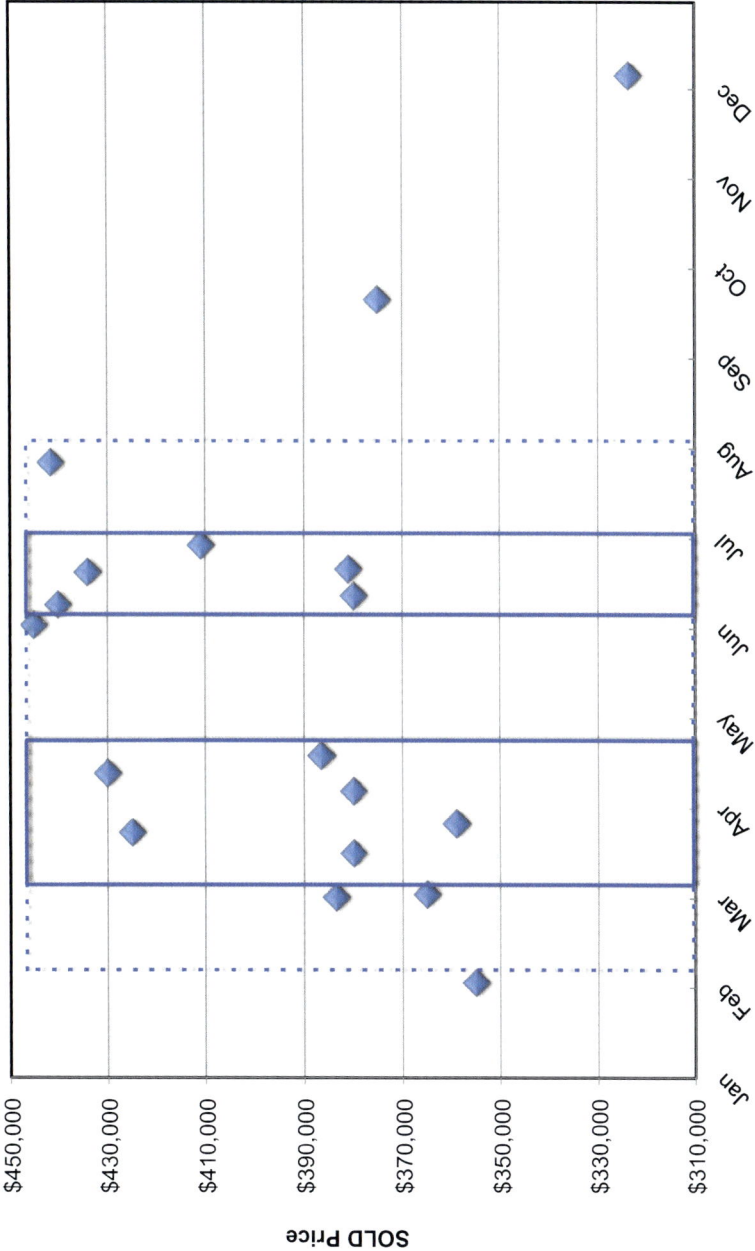

SOLD Price

SOLD Date

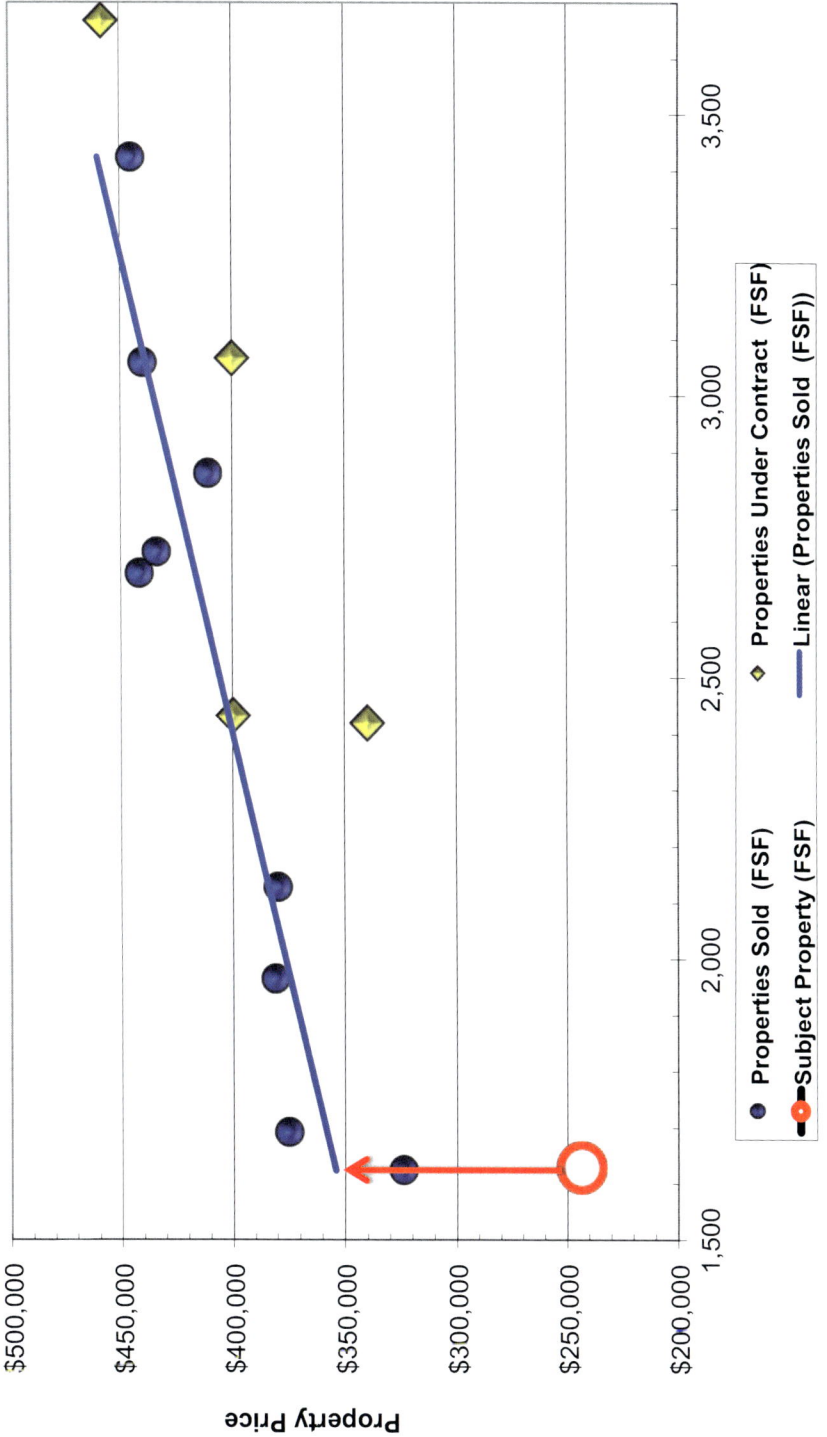

Activity in English Ranch (Fort Collins)
Property Price vs. Finished Square Feet (FSF); From 2/29/08 to 12/6/16

About the Author

Tim DeLeon was born July 31, 1954, in Pueblo, Colorado. Tim entered real estate following a twenty-five-year career at Hewlett-Packard, developing software products. He found that he loved real estate but that there was no software out there to really help a person accurately price a home and then show a customer why. Embracing the motto of "Showing is better than telling!" Tim created Scattergram Pricing. Soon after, he created the Neighborhood Buying Patterns and the rest of the tools that now make up the Visual Pricing System.

Using the tools to create success in his own real estate career, Tim is now helping thousands of real estate agents across the nation by providing quality tools and education that help price homes accurately, and quickly.

To learn more about Tim or the Focus 1st LLC tools, please visit:

www.focus1st.com

Made in the USA
Columbia, SC
21 April 2020